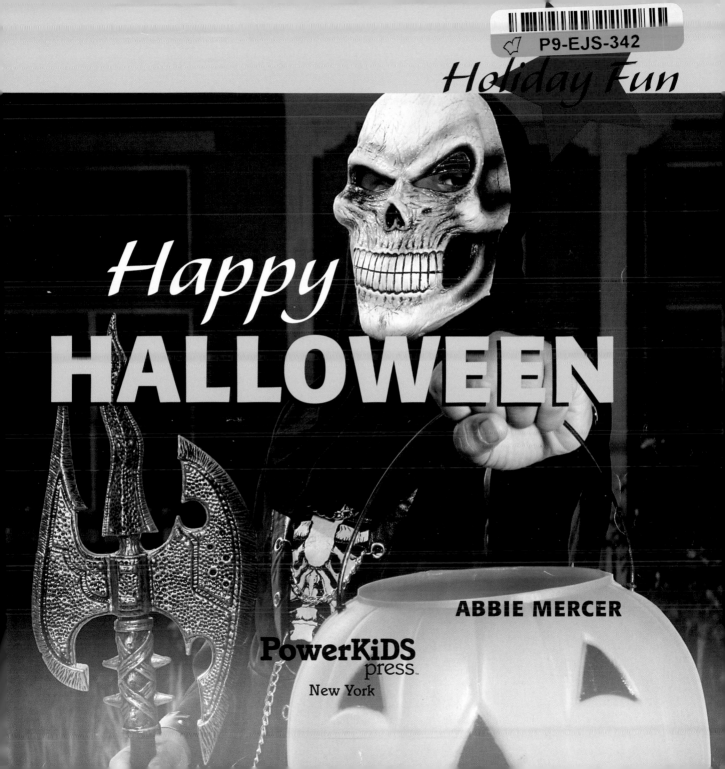

Happy HALLOWEEN

ABBIE MERCER

PowerKiDS press
New York

For Yvonne Hsi and Suzy Snell

Published in 2008 by The Rosen Publishing Group, Inc.
29 East 21st Street, New York, NY 10010

First Edition

Editor: Amelie von Zumbusch
Book Design: Julio Gil
Photo Researcher: Nicole Pristash

Photo Credits: Cover, pp. 1, 11, 17, 21 © Shutterstock.com; p. 5 © Mel Yates/Getty Images; p. 7 © www.istockphoto.com/Jim Jurica; p. 9 © Getty Images; p. 13 © AFP/Getty Images; p. 15 © www.istockphoto.com/Rob Sylvan; p. 19 © www.istockphoto.com/Bo Insogna.

Library of Congress Cataloging-in-Publication Data

Mercer, Abbie.
  Happy Halloween / Abbie Mercer.
      p. cm. — (Holiday fun)
  Includes index.
  ISBN-13: 978-1-4042-3806-0 (library binding)
  ISBN-10: 1-4042-3806-9 (library binding)
  1. Halloween costumes. I. Title.
  TT633.M47 2008
  646.4'78—dc22
                                          2006102681

Manufactured in the United States of America

Contents

What Is Halloween?

Halloween is a time for scary fun! This holiday comes every year on October 31. People **celebrate** Halloween by dressing up in **costumes**. They **decorate** their houses with scary things, like ghosts, black cats, and jack-o'-lanterns. People also tell scary stories and watch scary movies on Halloween.

Halloween is especially fun if you are a kid. This is because kids go trick-or-treating on Halloween. They wear costumes, visit their neighbors, and say "trick or treat." The neighbors give them a treat, such as candy, fruit, or money. Have you ever gone trick-or-treating?

These boys and girls are dressed up in their costumes to go trick-or-treating.

Halloween is based on a holiday, called **Samhain**, that the **Celts** celebrated thousands of years ago. The Celts believed the line between the living and the dead was erased on this day. It was a day when ghosts moved among the living. The Celts wore costumes and played tricks to scare away the ghosts.

Halloween **traditions** come from a **Christian** holiday called All Souls' Day, too. On All Souls' Day, people gave beggars cakes called soul cakes. The beggars promised to pray for the families of people who gave them cakes. This is how trick-or-treating started!

Today, trick-or-treaters get treats like candy instead of soul cakes.

Costumes, Masks, and Make-Up

Kids like trick-or-treating not only because they love getting treats, but also because it is fun to wear costumes. People dress up as many different things for Halloween. Some people dress up as something scary, such as a witch or a ghost. Not all Halloween costumes are scary, though. Many kids dress up as princesses, animals, or sports stars. Other people decide to be a character from their favorite book or movie.

Masks are part of some Halloween costumes. Other trick-or-treaters wear make-up. You can use make-up to make yourself a green-faced witch or a striped tiger.

This girl is having make-up put on so that she can be a clown for Halloween.

How to Make a Ghost Costume

It is lots of fun to make your own costume. One of the easiest Halloween costumes to make is a ghost costume.

1 Find an old, white sheet that no one needs anymore. Spread the sheet out on the ground.

2 Draw two circles just under the middle of the sheet. They will be the ghost's eyes. Cut the eyes out. Draw a mouth below the eyes.

3 Cut small holes on the right and left edges of the sheet. The holes should be a bit below the eyes.

4 Put the sheet over your head so that you can look through the eyeholes. Slide your fingers through the holes you made in step 3. Now you are a ghost, like the one on page 11.

Halloween Parades

It is fun to show off your Halloween costume. Many people show off their costumes by marching in parades. Schools often have parades so that kids can see how their classmates will dress up to go trick-or-treating.

Sometimes towns or cities hold parades. The world's biggest Halloween parade takes place in New York City's Greenwich Village. More than two million people go to this parade every year. Lots of dancers and people playing music march in the parade. The parade also has giant puppets on sticks. It takes a whole team of people to move just one puppet.

These kids are at a Halloween parade in Tokyo, Japan. Halloween parades take place all around the world.

Halloween Parties

Many people hold Halloween parties to celebrate this scary holiday. Sometimes these parties have a costume **contest**. Everyone who comes to the party wears a costume, and the people at the party vote on whose costume is the best. There are sometimes separate contests for the scariest costume, the funniest costume, and the most creative costume.

People also play games at Halloween parties. One Halloween game is bobbing for apples. To bob for apples, fill a tub with water and float some apples in it. Try to pick up one of the floating apples using just your mouth.

Bobbing for apples is fun, but picking up an apple with your teeth is harder than you may think!

How to Make Caramel Apples

Many people eat special Halloween treats at their Halloween parties. Caramel apples are a favorite Halloween treat.

1 Start by spreading wax paper over a cookie sheet. Then wash and dry four apples. Stick a Popsicle stick through the middle, or core, of each apple.

2 Put 11 ounces (312 g) of caramels in a microwave-safe bowl with 1 tablespoon (15 ml) of milk. Microwave the bowl for 2 minutes.

3 Use the Popsicle sticks to pick the apples up. Dip the apples in the bowl of melted caramel.

4 Put 1/2 cup (75 g) of cut-up nuts in a bowl. Dip the apples in the nuts and roll them around. Put the apples on the cookie sheet and into the refrigerator. Let them cool for 30 minutes. They should look like the apples on page 17.

Decorating for Halloween

Many people decorate their houses for Halloween. People like to make their houses look scary for the trick-or-treaters who visit them. People put pictures of scary things, like monsters, ghosts, witches, and black cats, in their windows. Some people play scary music or have creepy lights. Others set up imaginary **graveyards** in their gardens.

One of the best-liked Halloween decorations is the jack-o'-lantern. Jack-o'-lanterns are made from large, round vegetables called pumpkins. People make jack-o'-lanterns by cutting a face in the pumpkin and then setting a candle inside it. Jack-o'-lanterns can have scary, funny, or happy faces.

Many people put up spiderwebs made out of cotton to make their houses look scary for Halloween.

How to Make a Jack-o'-Lantern

Jack-o'-lanterns are lots of fun to make! However, make sure to ask an adult for help when you use a knife.

1

Use a knife to cut carefully around the pumpkin's stem. Take the top of the pumpkin off.

2

Use a strong spoon to clean out the inside of the pumpkin, like the girl on page 21.

3

Use a marker to draw a face on the pumpkin. Make sure to use closed shapes. Use a small knife to carefully cut along the lines you drew.

4

Put your pumpkin down where people can see it. Place a small, short candle inside the pumpkin. The kind of candles called tea lights work well. Have an adult light the candle for you. You have finished your jack-o'-lantern!

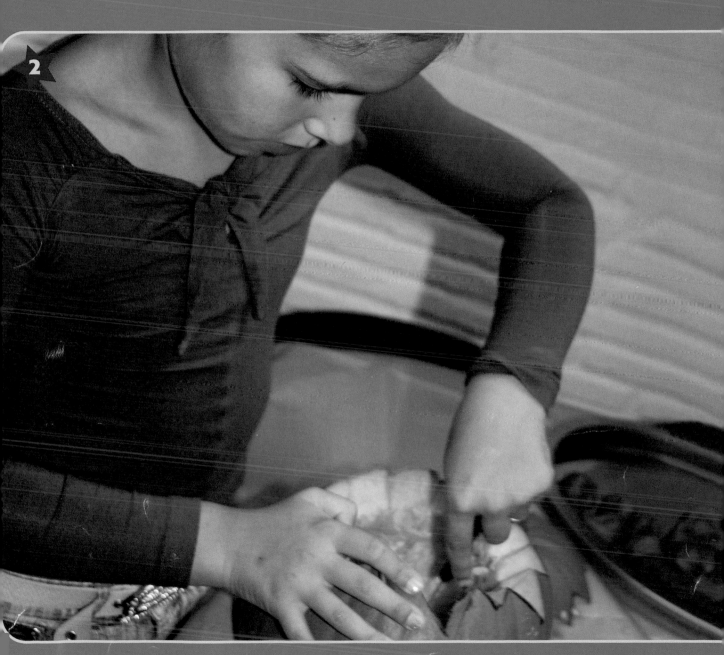

Halloween Traditions

Though Halloween is thousands of years old, people still create new Halloween traditions today. One Halloween tradition that has started lately is trick-or-treating at neighborhood stores. Many adults think it is unsafe for kids to go from house to house at night. Therefore, the stores in some cities and towns give out candy to trick-or-treaters. Stores are well lighted and have lots of people around to make sure the kids are safe.

Each family has its own Halloween traditions. Some families have Halloween parties every year. Other families set up a **haunted house**. What are your family's Halloween traditions?

Glossary

celebrate (SEH-luh-brayt) To honor an important moment by doing special things.

Celts (KELTS) Early European people who lived in the British Isles, France, Spain, and parts of Asia.

Christian (KRIS-chun) Having to do with people who follow the teachings of Jesus Christ and the Bible.

contest (KAHN-test) A game in which two or more people try to win.

costumes (KOS-toomz) Clothes that make a person look like someone or something else.

decorate (DEH-kuh-rayt) To add objects that make something prettier or more interesting.

graveyards (GRAYV-yahrdz) Places where dead people have been laid to rest.

haunted house (HONT-ed HOWS) A place with many scary things that people go through for fun.

Samhain (SOW-in) A holiday that honors the end of the old Celtic year.

traditions (truh-DIH-shunz) Ways of doing something that have been passed down over time.

Index

Web Sites

Due to the changing nature of Internet links, PowerKids Press has developed an online list of Web sites related to the subject of this book. This site is updated regularly. Please use this link to access the list:
www.powerkidslinks.com/hfun/hall/